ACE Group Fitness Specialty Book

Group Indoor Cycling

by Norma Shechtman, M. Ed., M.A.

CAUSEWAY
22 O'Meara St.
Ottawa, Ontario
K1Y 4N6

AMERICAN COUNCIL ON EXERCISE®
www.acefitness.org

Library of Congress Catalog Card Number: 00-104272

First edition
ISBN 1-890720-03-8
Copyright © 2000 American Council on Exercise® (ACE®)
Printed in the United States of America.

A B C D E F

Distributed by:
American Council on Exercise
P. O. Box 910449
San Diego, CA 92191-0449
(858) 535-8227
(858) 535-1778 (FAX)
www.acefitness.org

Managing Editor: Daniel Green
Design: Karen McGuire
Production: Glenn Valentine
Manager of Publications: Christine Ekeroth
Associate Editor: Joy Keller
Index: Bonny McLaughlin
Model: Theresa Schoppe

V-bike™ appearing in all photographs, and cover photograph of V-bike and Precision Cycling™ courtesy of Star Trac®.

Acknowledgements:
Thanks to the entire American Council on Exercise staff for their support and guidance through the process of creating this manual.

NOTICE
The fitness industry is ever-changing. As new research and clinical experience broaden our knowledge, changes in programming and standards are required. The authors and the publisher of this work have checked with sources believed to be reliable in their efforts to provide information that is complete and generally in accord with the standards accepted at the time of publication. However, in view of the possibility of human error or changes in industry standards, neither the authors nor the publisher nor any other party who has been involved in the preparation or publication of this work warrants that the information contained herein is in every respect accurate or complete, and they are not responsible for any errors or omissions or the results obtained from the use of such information. Readers are encouraged to confirm the information contained herein with other sources.

REVIEWERS

Lynne Brick is the president and founder of Brick Bodies Fitness Services. She owns a chain of six health clubs, has starred in over two dozen videos, authored five books, and is an internationally recognized speaker. Brick was named IDEA Fitness Instructor of the Year in 1990.

Robert Sherman is president and owner of F.I.T., Inc., a Bethesda, Md.–based corporation focusing on Cycle Reebok and personal and athletic training. Sherman is a program developer for Cycle Reebok, a Master Trainer for Reebok International Ltd., and conducts instructor training internationally and throughout the United States. Sherman was named as one of the foremost fitness trainers in America by Allure and was selected by the Washington Post as one of the best fitness instructors in the Washington, D.C., area. Sherman, a business school graduate of the University of Maryland, is gold certified by ACE, AFAA, and ACSM.

Jeffrey Vandiver is the founder and co-owner of Fitness A La Carte Productions, a fitness service and consulting company located in Beverley Hills, Calif. He has choreographed and starred in numerous fitness videos, and has been featured in fitness magazines in the United States, Japan, and Brazil. In 1990, Vandiver was the first World Aerobic Champion in the individual men's category at the World Aerobic Championships.

TABLE OF CONTENTS

INTRODUCTION

The American Council on Exercise (ACE) is pleased to include Group Indoor Cycling *as a Group Fitness Specialty Book. As the industry* continues to expand, evolve, and redefine itself, it is only natural that indoor cycling be recognized as a viable component of fitness. It has also become apparent that guidelines and criteria should be established so that this exercise modality can be practiced both safely and effectively. The intent of this book is to educate and give guidance to fitness professionals that wish to teach indoor cycling. As with all areas of fitness, education is a continual process. ACE recognizes this is a broad subject requiring serious study and we encourage you to use the References and Suggested Reading to further your knowledge.

Chapter One

Introduction to Indoor Cycling

For decades, indoor cycling has been used by cyclists wanting to train without having to fight inclement weather. Cycling clinics offer training on **rollers**, **trainers**, and stationary bikes, or on ergometers at home or in bicycle shops. Rollers help to develop pedal stroke, balance, and specific bike-handling skills, while trainers are used to practice various types of sprints that require shifting gears and the positioning of one's self on an actual bike. Stationary bikes are used to control and monitor **cadence** and workload, which are calculated with heart rate information to determine watts/workload/$\dot{V}O_2$ max. Together, these apparatus provide a complete training regimen for even the most avid cyclist.

Group indoor cycling has evolved into a fitness phenomenon. In the mid-1980s, Johnny Goldberg, who is better known as

Johnny G, partnered with Schwinn® to create Spinning® and develop a bike specifically for the program. This program, also known as Mad Dogg Athletics, was introduced to the fitness industry in 1995 and focuses on visualizing an outdoor ride, complete with wind, hills, and butterflies. The primary goal of Johnny G's program is empowerment. One year later both Keiser and Reebok developed their own programs. A team of group exercise specialists and scientists, including a biomechanist and sport psychologist, created Studio Cycling™ by Reebok (now known as Cycle Reebok™). Reebok's program is based on science, safety for the masses, detailed analysis of body alignment, and conservative exercise progression. Choreographer Karen Voight led a group of former dancers and group exercisers in the development of Power Pacing™ by Keiser, which is set apart by its emphasis on moving with musical rhythms, applying more body choreography (such as swaying), and incorporating upper-body exercise into rides.

Growth

Outdoor cycling activity has increased dramatically in recent years. According to figures available from the Sporting Goods Manufacturing Association, the number of Americans participating in mountain biking increased from 1.5 million in 1987 to 10.9 million in 1998. There is also a higher number of participants training indoors with a commitment to stay in shape and perfect their cycling techniques. In addition, there are individuals who prefer to train aerobically without adding stress to their joints, and indoor cycling fits this need. Indoor cycling programs can be adapted for a variety of populations and are currently being used successfully for individuals with spinal cord injuries, arthritis, and cerebral palsy, and as rehabilitation following surgery.

Benefits

Cycling is an excellent cardiorespiratory activity and a good alternative for those who do not like to jog or run, or who have orthopedic limitations to weightbearing exercise. The many physical benefits of indoor cycling include improved cardiorespiratory endurance, an increase in muscular strength and endurance, and a decrease of body fat and increase of lean body mass. It is also a great weight-management tool when used in conjunction with a well-balanced diet.

Psychological benefits include stress relief, an increase in beta-endorphins, and the enjoyment drawn from participating in a fun, social activity.

In addition to convenience, another advantage of indoor cycling is its relative safety, which can lead to a more intense workout. Distractions are minimized, allowing participants to focus on maximizing or maintaining heart rate for the session without worrying about cars, potholes, and other road hazards. The workout can also be more precise, since participants can lend more focus to the program.

There are a number of additional benefits to the indoor cycling format. Participants improve pedal stroke action by focusing on a smooth and complete pedal cycle on each leg independently. Also, participants achieve personalized workouts within a group setting by modifying resistance, cadence, and body position. Indoor cycling may also be used for recovery. By working at a lower intensity, riders enhance venous return and speed up lactic acid clearance from the muscle and diminish post-training stiffness and soreness.

Kinesiology

The main force in cycling comes from the hip and knee extensor muscles during the downward push. With the help of toe clips and conscious effort, the hip and dorsi-flexors are used to return the pedal to the up position.

Robert Gregor, Ph.D., and others from the University of California have identified the major cycling muscles of the leg using a technique called electromyography (EMG), which measures electrical impulses in contracting muscles (Burke, 1995). The unique advantage of EMG is that it reveals both the intensity and the duration of a muscle's action and provides the precise time sequence of muscular movement. EMGs show that many major lower-extremity muscles produce hip extension (propulsion), the driving force when cycling (Figure 1).

The gluteus maximus and biceps femoris play major roles in hip extension from 0 degrees at top dead center to 180 degrees at bottom dead center. The rectus femoris, vastus medialis, and vastus lateralis, the principle extensors of the knee, are active at the same time as the hamstrings: from 0 degrees to 75 degrees, and during the last 90 degrees of the recovery, helping to flex the hip. Their primary use is during the propulsion phase of the pedal stroke.

Knee extension and flexion are important in the production of force during cycling. The semimembranosus, biceps femoris, and

When describing pedal position, you can use either degrees or clock positions. For example, the first half of the pedal stroke, the propulsion phase, begins with the pedal at top dead center, twelve o'clock or 0 degrees, and ends at bottom dead center, six o'clock or 180 degrees. The second half of the pedal stroke, the recovery phase, begins at six o'clock and ends back at twelve o'clock.

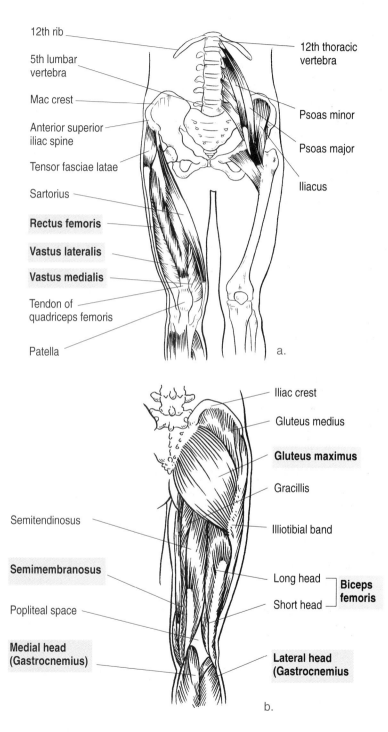

12th rib

5th lumbar vertebra

Mac crest

Anterior superior iliac spine

Tensor fasciae latae

Sartorius

Rectus femoris

Vastus lateralis

Vastus medialis

Tendon of quadriceps femoris

Patella

12th thoracic vertebra

Psoas minor

Psoas major

Iliacus

a.

Iliac crest

Gluteus medius

Gluteus maximus

Gracillis

Illiotibial band

Semitendinosus

Semimembranosus

Popliteal space

Medial head (Gastrocnemius)

Long head

Short head

Biceps femoris

Lateral head (Gastrocnemius

b.

Figure 1

a. Anterior musculature of the hip and knee, prime movers for hip flexion (iliacus, psoas major and minor) and knee extension.

b. Posterior musculature of the hip and knee, prime movers for hip extension (gluteus maximus and hamstrings) and knee flexion (hamstrings and gastrocnemius).

gastrocnemius play a role in knee flexion. To complement the cycling, participants need to follow a strength-training program that works both the knee flexors and knee extensors.

Results attained by Gregor et al. from measures of pedal force and from high-speed filming, show that pedal position varies from almost horizontal at two o'clock to slightly heel-down at three o'clock (Figure 2b). A maximum toes-down position is reached at about 75 degrees before top dead center. The pattern suggested in Figure 2a is both anatomically and mechanically impossible if the rider remains in the saddle. According to Burke, the ankling pattern of the cyclist (movement of the ankle from dorsiflexion through plantar flexion), should look like that in Figure 2b. Following this pattern increases the effective force on the pedal by pushing through at the top of the stroke and pulling back at the bottom (Burke, 1995).

The foot should be positioned so that the ball of the foot is directly over the pedal axle. To avoid knee pain, cleats should be adjusted so that the foot rests on the pedal naturally. Experienced cyclists set their cleats with a rotational adjustment device at their local bicycle shops. Most cyclists use clipless pedals that allow the foot to "float" a few degrees inward or outward on the pedal as it moves through the pedal cycle. Research has shown that these new pedal systems put less strain on the knee and allow a more natural pedaling motion. The floating-pedal systems allow the tibia to move in and rotate as riders push down on the pedal. In a fixed-pedal system, the knee and its ligaments absorb much of this rotation, which can potentially cause knee problems (Burke, 1995).

According to Burke, the movements at the hip, knee, and ankle during the downward portion, or power phase, of the pedal stroke

a.

Figure 2
a. The ankling pattern that is recommended in popular bicycling literature, but is both anatomically and mechanically impossible.

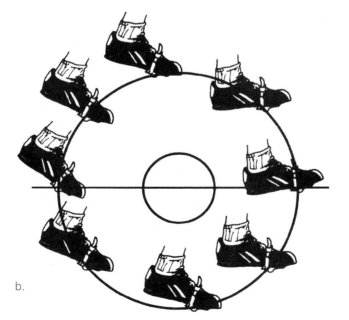

b.

b. Preferred ankling pattern, in which you can increase your effective force by pushing through at the top of your stroke and pulling back at the bottom.

(Reprinted with permission from Burke, 1995.)

consist of simultaneous extension of the hip and knee along with some plantar flexion of the ankle. This is followed by the upstroke, commonly called the recovery phase, which involves simultaneous flexion of the hip and knee along with continued plantar flexion of the ankle. While it is clear that the muscles responsible for hip and knee extension generate the majority of the force that drives the bicycle, the precise role of the plantar flexors of the ankle remains obscure. When interviewed, off-road cyclists report that during the power phase they perceived active plantar flexion and that during the upstroke (recovery) their ankles were relaxed (Burke, 1995).

Chapter Two

Teaching an Indoor Cycling Class

Equipment

Participants need a few items to provide comfort and increase efficiency throughout the ride (Figure 3). Each participant needs a pair of padded bike shorts and/or a soft padded seat to prevent saddle soreness. The primary function of the shorts is to reduce friction caused by moisture on the skin. Suitable footwear, apparel, and a well-designed stationary cycle are also important for the safety and effectiveness of a good cycling program.

A low-cut shoe, which allows greater range of motion about the ankle, works best. Athletic or cycling shoes that have the appropriate cleat to match the pedal may also be used. The most common cleats are LOOK and SPD (Figure 4).

A stiff-soled shoe is essential, as soft-soled shoes will bend over the pedal while a rider is standing and may make the feet numb. Shoes must be strapped snugly into the cages to prevent feet from coming out during class, and shoelaces should be tucked in to prevent tangling around the crank arm or pedal. If clipless pedals are used, check the tension on the pedals to make sure cleats and shoes are aligned. Improper cleat alignment can cause undue stress on ligaments, tendons, and muscles.

Clothing should be lightweight, fit comfortably, and enhance the cooling effect for thermoregulation of the body. Cycling gloves may help those with sensitive hands, but are not required. It is extremely important that each participant has his or her own water bottle to rehydrate before, during, and after class.

Figure 3
Basic equipment includes padded bike shorts, water bottle, and towel.

Figure 4a
LOOK cleats

a.

Figure 4b
SPD cleats

b.

The room or area in which the class is conducted should be well ventilated to create air circulation for evaporation.

The Bike

There are several bikes on the market, each with different adjustments and pedals (Figure 5). Before teaching any group indoor cycling class, familiarize yourself with the bikes being used, paying special attention to safety features.

Bike Set-up

Proper bike fit is essential to the success and longevity of a cycling program. Riders must be positioned correctly so they are comfortable in the saddle. Ensuring correct knee and hip alignment is necessary for preventing stress injuries. Check and recheck participants' fit on the bike by looking at key areas. Is there a slight bend in the leg that is dropped down to a six o'clock position? Are elbows slightly bent when participants are in an upright position on the bike? Do the participants have a hunched look in their backs or are they in a neutral spinal position? Overall, do they look relaxed and comfortable on their bikes? Sometimes it takes a few sessions and numerous adjustments to find that perfect fit. After all adjustments, pop pins should be completely engaged and locked in place.

Checking with participants the next day is a good way to find out if there were any discomforts or unusual pains from the ride. These issues should be addressed prior to each class. Recommend that new participants take a short ride for their first class; most clubs and studios offer an introductory class for new participants. Limiting themselves to a ride of 20 to 30 minutes for their first class allows participants to feel successful and walk away with a pleasant experience.

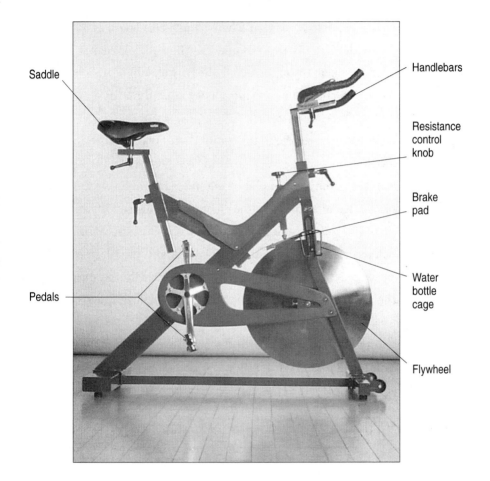

Figure 5
The bike
and its
components

Saddle

Handlebars

Resistance
control
knob

Brake
pad

Water
bottle
cage

Pedals

Flywheel

Positioning the height of the seat post

Have participants stand next to their bikes. Start by placing the saddle approximately at the hip or about two inches down from the hipbone. Then, have them sit on the saddle and extend one leg down to a six o'clock position. There should be a slight bend in the knee (greater than 10 degrees and less than 40 degrees of flexion) as the foot sits on top of the pedal; the heel should be able to drop slightly. Also, check that one hip is not higher than the other.

Positioning the seat fore and aft

Begin with the saddle in the center position and then adjust accordingly. Check arm extension at the furthest end of the handlebars. If the arms are completely extended, move the seat closer. If there is too much bend in the elbows, push the saddle back. Another useful measurement is to place the feet at three and nine o'clock (cranks parallel to the floor). Look at a plumb line dropped from the patella — it should intersect with the shoe strap on the pedal (over the instep of the foot or middle of the foot).

Handlebar adjustment

Beginners should start with the handlebars at or above saddle height. Participants with back problems should begin with their handlebars as high as possible.

Technique

Pedaling Technique

According to Dr. Burke (1995), the first thing to consider in pedaling technique is the shape of the stroke. Most people get on the bike and pedal by pushing down forcefully and resting on the upstroke. Unfortunately, pushing down on the pedals eliminates all the power of the other muscle groups in the legs, the calves and hamstrings. Not using these muscles delivers less power to the bike and the thighs will tire more quickly.

Only pushing down on the pedals creates a very short, uneven stroke and limits the momentum of the pedaling stroke with each revolution. Instructors have been known to say "pull up" on the pedals, using the toe clips or clipless pedals, in order to recruit other leg muscles. However, the force applied by a rider pulling up is primarily directed to the back. Additionally, there is only a minute amount of force achieved, which plays a small role in helping performance.

So, what is the better pedaling stroke? Unfortunately, a good pedaling stroke is not easy to acquire and takes a lot of practice. Basically, riders should pull back as they ride through the beginning of the upstroke. This is not the same as pulling up, as riders should pull back starting at the five to six o'clock portion of the stroke to about the seven o'clock position. In other words, the force is applied across the bottom of the down stroke. Pulling back involves all of the lower leg muscles in the motion and makes it possible to apply power for a longer period in the upstroke. More importantly, this will create a smooth transition from up to down stroke. This is not a natural movement and must be practiced.

One of the most important aspects of good pedaling technique is being correctly fitted on the bike. Incorrect overall height or pedaling position makes it difficult to reach optimum efficiency in the pedaling technique. Participants will find that their riding will improve when they combine pulling back on the pedals with a correct overall height and pedaling position. Soon, their pedaling style will be more fluid and involve more of their leg muscles.

Body Positioning

Hand Positions

Hand positions utilized in indoor cycling replicate those in road cycling. Each hand position is used for specific parts of the ride. There are three main hand positions.

The first position is a closed and center position used for seated flat rides with light resistance, as during the warm-up, cool-down, and recovery portions of the class (Figure 6). The hands rest lightly on the center of the bars and are touching each other.

The second position is wider, with the hands resting lightly on the straight part of the handlebars (Figure 7). This position is used for seated climbs, standing jogs or runs, seated sprints, and moving in and out of the saddle.

The third position is with hands extended to the ends of the bars and is used mainly for a very steep climb with heavy resistance (Figure 8). Arms in this position should not be too extended, maintaining a slight bend in the elbow.

Figure 6
The closed and center hand position, used for seated flat rides with light resistance.

Figure 7
Wider hand position, used for seated climbs, standing jogs or runs, seated sprints, and moving in and out of the saddle.

Figure 8
Position with hands extended to the ends of the bars, used for very steep climbs with heavy resistance.

The main rule to remember in all of these positions is to keep the wrists in a neutral position. Remind participants to keep the grip on the handlebars relaxed by wiggling the fingers and to change the hand positions frequently, even if it is only slightly.

Seated Positions

Flats — Minimal resistance; moderate-to-high revolutions per minute (rpms)

This is a basic cycling technique used during the warm-up, cool-down, and recovery periods. This technique helps to build stamina and smooth pedal strokes, and is considered a baseline position for a rider's initial training. This position allows for lactate clearance and cardiorespiratory recovery, and is a way to reestablish the basic pedal stroke following a high-intensity section of class. Hands are usually in the center closed grip position

Figure 9
Proper spinal alignment on a flat; neutral position.

with a light touch on the handlebars. Elbows and shoulders are relaxed and the head is in line with a neutral spine. Remind participants to keep the chest expanded to ensure that the lungs are open, and to avoid bouncing in the seat. Knees should remain in line with the toes while the feet are in a neutral position (Figures 9 & 10). Encourage beginners to return to this

Figure 10
a. Improper spinal alignment; arched back.

b. Improper spinal alignment; rounded back.

position when they are tired or can not keep up with the class. The visualization for this section of class would be riding along flat roads, as in a valley or on a plateau.

Climbing — Moderate-to-heavy resistance; moderate-to-lower rpms

Climbing involves pedaling with increased resistance and a slower cadence. Intensity increases, as this technique promotes greater lower-body strength and endurance and increases the demand on the cardiorespiratory system. Hands are positioned wider on the handlebars for stability and to open the chest cavity for breathing. Elbows and shoulders are relaxed with the head in line with the spine. Shoulders should be retracted and depressed, not rounded. Since this is a very intense movement, it is important to cue relaxation techniques to release tension in the upper body. Shifting the buttocks to the back of the saddle allows for more power and more recruitment of the gluteal muscles. Dropping the heels on the down stroke increases the recruitment of the hamstrings and calves. If there is a "push and pull" or squaring of the pedal stroke, resistance may be too high. The hands may add a slight push or pull motion to the handlebars without a tight grip, keeping the fingers relaxed. Remind participants to keep a long neck and neutral position of the spine (Figures 11 & 12).

Figure 11
Proper position for climbing, with long neck and neutral position of the spine.

Figure 12
Improper
climbing
position.

Sprints — Light-to-moderate resistance; high rpms

In this advanced technique, the hands are in the wider position on the handlebars with the elbows and shoulders relaxed. Speedwork is very challenging and takes a lot of practice and skill. Pedaling stroke should be smooth, fluid, and free from bouncing. Be sure that there is always some resistance on the flywheel to avoid losing pedaling control (Figures 13 & 14).

Figure 13
Proper position for sprints.

Figure 14

Improper position for sprints.

One-legged drills — Variable resistance

Instruct participants to feel the difference between leading with one leg or the other to practice smoothing out the pedal stroke. By visualizing and continuing to cycle with both feet in the pedals, focus on leading with one leg and just allow the other leg to follow. Slowly increase the resistance to force that lead leg to work harder. After a specific amount of time apply the same drill to the other leg. To culminate the drill, work both legs together to smooth out the pedal stroke.

Standing Positions

Standing on a flat — Moderate resistance

In this position, the torso is lifted to an upright position with slight hip flexion. With knees slightly flexed and the rider's center of gravity balanced over the cranks, lift the chest and place the hands in a wide position with a light touch. This position releases tension in the lower back and shoulders. Instruct participants to avoid leaning on the handlebars (Figures 15 & 16).

Figure 15
Proper form for standing on a flat, with center of gravity balanced over the cranks.

Figure 16
Improper
form for
standing
on a flat.

Standing jog/run/sprint — Variable resistance

When in a standing jog, position hands far apart for stability and to help breathing by keeping the lungs open, but keep a light touch on the handlebars. Relax the elbows and shoulders and balance your body weight over the center of the bike or the pedals. Position the hips over the saddle and keep the chest held upright. The tip of the saddle may brush the back of the legs. While in an out-of-saddle position, **leg speed** easily increases and the focus must be on controlling the speed. Avoid choppy, bouncy strokes by keeping the ball of the foot weighted on the pedal with slight pressure on the forefoot. Keep the torso stable without moving from side to side and the hips over the saddle tip (Figures 17 & 18).

Figure 17
Proper form for a standing jog, with the body weight balanced over the center of the bike and the chest held upright.

Figure 18
Improper
form for a
standing jog.

Standing climb — Moderate-to-heavy resistance

When leading a class through standing climbs, warn participants that too much resistance forces the body to "fight the bike" and may lead to potential injuries due to overtraining. Reach out to the extended position or to the ends of the handlebars and center body weight over the pedals with the tailbone over the saddle tip. The hip and knee positions have more flexion than in the standing jog and the hips slide back over the saddle. Keep elbows and shoulders relaxed and avoid constricting the lungs and rounding the back.

Keep the back extended and abdominals pulled in, and allow the torso to shift slightly with the downstroke (Figures 19 & 20).

Figure 19
Proper form for standing climb, with the back extended and abdominals contracted.

Figure 20
Improper form for standing climb.

Stand and sit, lift, or jump — Moderate resistance

With hands in a wide position, the body is lifted upright and off the saddle, and then returned to the saddle. The weight is entirely on the feet, and the hands are used only for balance and safety when out of the saddle. The weight is shifted to the saddle during the seated phase of the movement. In outdoor cycling, riders lift out of the saddle for brief periods of time when taking a steep turn, avoiding a rock, or accelerating to a faster speed. In indoor cycling, this movement is simulated to work on coordination and explosive strength, work the front of the leg, and encourage postural awareness. The upper body stays relaxed as the body weight is lifted from the saddle. Remind participants to control the movement and avoid bouncing in and out of the saddle.

Teaching Techniques

- Arrive at least 15 minutes early.
- Have your music cued up and ready to play.
- Set up your bike.
- Put on your shoes.
- Have a water bottle and towel.
- Be available to help newer participants set up their bikes.
- Wear proper indoor cycling gear (padded bike shorts and a cool shirt) and suggest that participants do the same.
- Use music you and your participants will enjoy. Professional tapes are available and have proper licensing.
- Encourage your participants to cross train to work other muscle groups and avoid overuse injuries.
- Create sensible rides and give participants time to perfect the movement. Quick changes are disruptive and frustrating to the participants.
- Give participants tips to modify their ride.

When lowering from an out-of-saddle position, reduce the resistance slightly, maintain or increase speed, and lower the body gently. This is an advanced technique because it requires a higher degree of lower-body strength, torso stabilization, balance, and coordination (Figures 21 & 22).

Figure 21
Proper form to stand and sit, lift, or jump, focusing on lower-body strength, torso stabilization, balance, and coordination.

Figure 22
Improper form to stand and sit, lift, or jump.

Cueing and Visualization

Verbal cues need to be clear and precise, and reminders should be positive and communicate constructive feedback. Remember, you are there for support, education, and motivation. Use verbal instructions for body position, pedal stroke, specifying muscles used, breathing, and visualization. During body alignment cues, participants can focus their attention on their bodies and neutral alignment.

Give frequent reminders about pedaling techniques and initiate muscle focus through good cues. For example, when climbing, instruct participants to feel the hamstrings and gluteal muscles engaging to ride up the hill by directing their attention to the specific muscle group and focus internally. Closing the eyes and actually visualizing a hill aids in getting that "feel" of a hill.

Deep, rhythmic breathing also can help participants focus internally and pay attention to alignment, pedal stroke, and specific muscles that are being used.

In addition to focusing on a specific muscle group, visualization also can help riders feel as though they are outdoors, which may increase performance and skill. Many athletes have improved their performance through visualization techniques. Visualization can be used before, during, and after the class, as in the cool-down period. For example, you can describe the feeling of completing a steep hill and the feeling of accomplishment that comes with this success. To increase speed, you might describe a chase and ask the participants to be the first to the end of the road. Visualization can also help participants be distracted from a difficult segment of the class. Creating a pleasant visual scene may help participants become more relaxed for the difficult segment. If an individual needs specific corrections, try to get off your bike and remove the microphone before giving a correction or specific cue.

Intensity Monitoring

It has been suggested that ratings of perceived exertion (RPE) may not be as reliable in cycling as in other activities when monitoring general exercise intensity, especially at higher workloads and lower rpms.

One good method of monitoring intensity during class is to use heart rate monitors (Figure 23). Many cyclists and trainers feel the heart rate monitor is a perfect coaching tool in that it allows users to observe heart rate changes without stopping the workout to take a manual pulse. Immediate feedback from the moni-

Figure 23
Heart rate
monitor.

tor can help motivate and regulate a workout. However, remind each participant to listen to his or her own body, and adjust the workout intensity accordingly.

Injury Prevention

The keys to injury prevention are good body positioning and proper bike adjustments. Hydration and ventilation are also essential for a safe and effective workout.

Postural breaks are very important, especially with beginners. The forward flexed position of the spine can become very uncomfortable. Periodic breaks to stretch the back can alleviate aches and pains and allow the participants to complete the class comfortably.

Every participant must learn how to handle loss of control of the pedals. If participants are pedaling too fast, they should know how to slow down the cadence and stop quickly on that particular bike. Each bike manufacturer is different and you must review this at the beginning of each class. Also, if one foot accidentally slips out of a pedal, the participant must react quickly and open the legs so as not to get hit in the shins by a pedal, and then stop the bike. Practice this in slow motion with new participants.

Troubleshooting

Numb hands

When participants grip the handlebars too tightly, circulation can be cut off and numbness may occur. Remind participants to

Safety Tips for Participants

- Cycling shoes are highly recommended.
- If you wear athletic shoes, be sure the shoelaces are tied so they are not in the way.
- If your feet come out of the pedals, immediately move your legs out to the side and stop the bike.
- To stop quickly, pull up on the tension dial, or push down on the flywheel resistance dial.
- Seat position: Adjust seat height so knees do not lock when the leg is straight; knees should not be in more than 90 degrees of flexion when the thigh is parallel to the floor. Adjust seat distance so the upper body is not flexed too far forward.
- Handlebar position: for newcomers, adjust bars even to or slightly higher than the seat. As one becomes more advanced, the handlebars can be positioned lower than the seat.
- Make sure your towel is not hanging over the flywheel.
- Padded cycling shorts will provide the best comfort and cushion.
- Arrive at least five minutes early to set up on the bike or get help from the instructor.
- Take it easy the first few times, go at your own pace, monitor your intensity, and compete only against yourself.
- Towels are mandatory. Please towel off your bike after class.
- Have fun, relax, and enjoy your ride!

relax the hands and rest them gently on the handlebars and bend their elbows to release pressure. Also, remind them to avoid inverted positions of the hands (palms facing inward), thumbs extended, or wrists flexed with weightbearing on the wrist or heel of the hand.

Sore buttocks

Bike shorts, padded briefs, or a padded seat cover are helpful. Beginning riders' buttocks may get sore until their legs become conditioned to prevent all of their body weight from resting on their buttocks.

Numb or sore feet

Numb or sore feet may be caused by toe straps that are too tight, feet jammed into the cage too far, or clenched toes. Instruct participants to wiggle their toes during the ride and check to see if the toe straps are too tight.

Sore backs

Hunching over and not maintaining a neutral position of the spine can lead to a sore back. Remind participants to take postural breaks throughout the class.

Personal Limitations

Classes that attract and retain participants with special needs have a larger potential participant base than programs catering only to the very fit. To successfully design classes for participants with special needs, you must provide specific instruction regarding overall intensity, cadence, resistance, and other modifications. In many cases, this will mean encouraging participants with medical conditions to ride "smarter, not harder."

Research has shown that a typical indoor cycling workout evokes an average heart rate response of 87% of maximum and an average $\dot{V}O_2$ response of 74% of maximum (Stavig, Francis, &

Buono, 1998). While this is good news for those capable of a high-intensity workout, those with lower functional capacities and/or special medical concerns require modifications in class design and instruction. To participate safely, participants with special needs must be given clear instruction with regards to intensity of effort and other considerations unique to their conditions.

Hypertension

Indoor cycling is an effective exercise for those with hypertension, provided that the overall intensity remains at the lower end of the heart rate training zone, which is at or below 60% of cardiac reserve. Although heart rate monitors are frequently used in cycling classes, percentages based on an age-predicted maximum do not correspond well with actual effort for participants who are taking antihypertensive agents, beta blockers, or calcium channel blockers. If a graded exercise test was given while the participant was on antihypertensive agents, the maximum heart rate achieved during that test can be used to calculate target rates. However, RPE must be monitored as well, since maximum achievable heart rates during group indoor cycling are lower than those achievable during treadmill walking on a graded exercise test.

If a participant is on vasodilators, which can increase heart rate response, he or she is more prone to hypotension and peripheral pooling of the blood, especially after exercise. These participants should gradually decrease resistance during recovery intervals and gently cool down at the end of class to avoid dizziness, fainting, or nausea.

Participants taking diuretics may be more prone to dehydration, as indoor cyclists generally lose high quantities of water through sweat. Always encourage all participants to drink plenty of water before, during, and after class.

Participants with high blood pressure should be careful not to clench the handlebars while riding, as this can exaggerate the blood pressure response. In a group setting it is difficult to monitor blood pressure readings. Therefore, have these participants avoid high-intensity cycling drills that may cause an exaggerated blood pressure response.

Pregnancy

Although each woman is unique, all pregnant women need to decrease their absolute workload (resistance and/or cadence) as their pregnancy advances. The American College of Obstetricians and Gynecologists (ACOG) recommends "mild to moderate" exercise intensity, but adds that highly trained women may be able to maintain higher intensities in the earlier stages of pregnancy (ACOG, 1994). Women who start indoor cycling after becoming pregnant must begin at low intensities and should not significantly increase their workload throughout term. Due to the variability in heart rate response to exercise during pregnancy, intensity should be cued by RPE. ACOG recommends that pregnant women avoid exercising to the point of exhaustion. If a pregnant woman shows signs of increased fatigue after riding, she should be advised to decrease intensity, frequency, or both. Encourage pregnant riders to eat a light, pre-exercise snack to avoid hypoglycemia, wear lightweight clothing, ride in a location where there is cool, circulating air, and drink plenty of fluids.

As pregnancy continues, the hips and knees will need to rotate outward during cycling to accommodate the larger belly. Sometimes, just slightly rotating the cleat on the cycling shoe can help keep the knees aligned over the toes. Pregnant women generally feel more comfortable with the handlebars fully raised. As the pelvis widens, many women need a wider and more comfortable saddle. Weight

gain in the abdomen can cause increased lumbar lordosis and sub-
sequent low back pain. Since forward flexion on the bike may add to
this discomfort, it is important to include frequent "postural breaks."
Increased weight in the abdomen tends to pull pregnant riders far-
ther forward over the pedals during standing drills, making the
knees more vulnerable to injury. Only use standing drills to the
extent that pregnant participants can perform them with proper
technique while putting minimum weight on the handlebars. Also
watch for "bottoming out," or fully extending the knee when standing. This can cause knee hyperextension, especially during pregnancy when hormonal changes increase joint laxity.

Pregnant women are generally cautioned not to cycle outdoors
due to risks associated with falling and often feel more comfortable
on a stationary bike. Provided a physician has found no contraindi-
cations to exercise, pregnant women can continue to enjoy indoor
cycling as long as there are no problems or warning signs, including
bleeding, pain, or discomfort.

Diabetes

Type 2 diabetes, which is highly associated with obesity, ac-
counts for the vast majority of all cases of diabetes. Individuals
with this condition can safely participate in indoor cycling classes and reap the benefits. New riders with diabetes should record
their pre- and postexercise blood glucose response to a given cycling class. These readings will help determine the most appropriate routine to help balance medication, meals, and exercise.
When designing a class to meet the needs of deconditioned participants with type 2 diabetes, avoid drills that provoke exces-
sive leg fatigue.

Many individuals with type 1 diabetes can attain high fitness
levels and participate in competitive athletics. However, the risk

of hyperglycemia increases with high-intensity exercise and exercise lasting longer than 20 to 30 minutes. Keep a watchful eye for signs of developing problems and be sure to keep some simple carbohydrate sources, such as fruit juices, readily available.

Arthritis

The two most common arthritic conditions are osteoarthritis (a degenerative joint disease) and rheumatoid arthritis (an inflammatory, multisystemic disease). Individuals with either type of arthritis can benefit from indoor cycling. Unfortunately, these

Teaching Guidelines

1. Ensure proper ventilation. If necessary, a fan can provide adequate cross ventilation to enable good evaporative heat loss. Unlike outdoor bicycling, indoor cycling requires adequate ventilation for prolonged exercise.

2. Remind beginning students to hold pedal crank speed relatively constant in the range of 70 rpm to 90 rpm per leg. Eventually, leg speed may get as high as 130 to 140 rpms, when an advanced cyclist is in a sprint.

3. Always warm up and cool down with five to 10 minutes of low-resistance cycling.

4. Before starting class, be sure to ask if there are any new participants. Make sure that all of the participants are set up properly on their bikes.

5. Review the safety features on the bike, remembering that some students may not be familiar with the type of bike used in your class. Demonstrate how to use the emergency brake. If a foot comes out of the cage or off the pedal, legs should be separated and pulled away from the pedals so the pedals do not hit the shins.

6. Remind participants to check their shoelaces to make sure they are tucked inside the shoe and not loose.

7. Always instruct participants to go at their own pace and listen to their bodies.

individuals often decrease physical activity because of joint pain, and consequently suffer from muscle atrophy and weakness, and loss of flexibility and joint range of motion.

In an indoor cycling class, the goals for riders with arthritis are generally to improve functional capacity, maintain or improve joint function, and protect joint structures from further damage. Riders whose knees and hips are arthritic may have diminished ability to perform rapid, repetitive movements with their legs. Exercise tolerance will vary depending on functional classification and whether or not the joints are inflamed. Reduce both intensity and duration during the initial phase of conditioning. Frequent changes in hand position, posture breaks, and a decreased work-load can help riders with arthritis. Changes in position may be beneficial when teaching participants with arthritis. For example, riders with arthritis of the spine may be better able to maintain a neutral position with the handlebars fully raised. Frequent breaks are also helpful. Riders with rheumatoid arthritis in the hands and fingers should be cautioned against tightly gripping the handlebars. After class, participants with arthritis should partici-pate in cool-down and flexibility work that targets the muscles and joints involved in cycling. You should also suggest participants perform daily full-body stretches and range-of-motion exercises.

Regardless of whether your class includes participants with health limitations, the level of resistance should be sufficient to enable partici-pants to retain control of the pedals throughout the entire revolution. Jeanne Nichols, Ph.D., professor of exercise science at San Diego State University and a nationally ranked master cyclist, finds that using the cue "preferred cadence" helps riders find the proper combination of resistance and cadence for their ability, while decreasing the impression that faster is always better.

Chapter Three

Programming

Components/Format of the Cycle Class

Cycle classes are usually 45 to 60 minutes long. The first 10 minutes is a warm-up and the last five to 10 minutes are used to cool down. This leaves about 25 to 40 minutes for a variety of profiles or a planned program. The first step is to establish the goals for the ride. The order and **tempo** of the music and the profile need to be planned before each class.

The warm-up usually starts gradually with little resistance, with the riders pedaling at a moderate speed. Use this time to review safety procedures, postural alignment, and hand positions, and offer the general statement that the workout is for each participant and competition with each other is not necessary. This portion of the class allows time for the body to gradually warm up, physically and emotionally. The heart rate will gradually elevate and there is a systemic, overall preparation for the upcoming session of indoor cycling.

After about 10 minutes, the main part of the ride can begin. Certain songs can be programmed to match your desire to start a climb, stay on a flat, increase speed, or jog out of the saddle. The following 25 to 40 minutes will vary from class to class. An organized profile needs to be established.

The last part of the class will bring the heart rate down, slow down the leg speed, decrease resistance, and gradually cool down the riders. This leads directly into a stretch of the major muscle groups that were used during the ride. Provide modifications for participants who may not be able to perform the stretches as pictured (Figures 24 through 30). If space allows, perform stretches off the bike.

Figure 24
Hamstring stretch.

Figure 25

Calf stretch. To avoid slipping, participants should remove their shoes prior to performing this stretch.

Figure 26
Back
stretch.

Figure 27
Quadriceps
stretch.

Figure 28
Chest
stretch.

Figure 29
Triceps
stretch.

Figure 30
Lateral
hip stretch.

Sample Class Formats

Endurance Workout

This type of class involves working in a moderate heart-rate zone for a long period of time, thereby helping to increase cardiovascular endurance.

5–10 minutes	1–2 songs	Warm-up, with music that is rhythmic and relaxed. Light resistance on the bike. Loosen up the legs, concentrate on posture, breathing, and systemically getting the body and mind ready for the ride.
2 minutes	1 song	Increase leg speed and gradually add more resistance.
2 minutes		Add more resistance while keeping the same leg speed.
2 minutes		Add more resistance while keeping the same leg speed.
2 minutes		Resistance decreases, **spin** out legs.
5–6 minutes	1 song	Stand up out of the saddle with moderate resistance. Song should have a strong beat that can be followed while standing. Have participants keep weight in torso, not on hands.
10–12 minutes	2 songs	Long seated spin with moderate resistance. Focus on form and have the participant feel the circle. Work on the pedal stroke to make it smooth and flowing.
5–6 minutes	1 song	Light resistance and quick speed. Use fun, upbeat music. Encourage participants to let go and enjoy the ride. Lifts in and out of the saddle can be used here: sprints of 30 sec-

		onds on and 30 seconds off, 1 minute rest, 30 second runs out of the saddle with 30 seconds seated in between.
5 minutes	1 song	Pre-cool-down — slow down the legs and continue the ride. There should be very little resistance on the bike. Use mellow music to relax the mind and body. Finish with stretches for the calves, hamstrings, quadriceps, hip flexors, shoulders, upper back, triceps, and neck. End with a cleansing breath and thank the participants for coming.

Strength Workout

An indoor cycling strength workout involves working in a moderate-to-high heart-rate zone. This helps increase muscular strength and power and cardiovascular endurance.

5–10 minutes	1–2 songs	Warm-up
10 minutes	2 songs	Increase resistance gradually. Work in the saddle and use strong driving music to help participants power into their strokes.
4–6 minutes	1 song	Hill work with increased resistance. Work in the saddle until the resistance slows down the pedal stroke so that participants need to stand and climb a steep hill.
5 minutes	1 song	Take most of the resistance off and just spin the legs to flush out the lactic acid and rejuvenate the legs. Music should be upbeat and fast-paced.
4–6 minutes	1 song	Moderate resistance with a lift on and off the saddle. Encourage participants to work with proper form

		both in and out of the saddle. Music should be strong and rhythmic.
3–5 minutes	1 song	Pretend that there is a paceline and they are following a leader. Establish high energy and an exciting, fast finish.
5 minutes	1 song	Pre-cool-down where participants are bringing down the intensity. Finish with a stretch off the bike.

Mixed Terrain Workout

These classes involve working in a variety of heart-rate zones, and varying intervals, speed work, and strength work.

5–10 minutes	1 song	Warm-up, with light resistance.
6 minutes	1 song	Hill climbing, increasing resistance very slowly. Start in the saddle and then go to a standing climb.
1 minute	1 song	Sprints, light resistance. (30 seconds on and 30 seconds off, 15 seconds on and 15 seconds off, repeat sequence and work with various intervals)
2 minutes	1 song	Moderate resistance, sitting.
30 seconds		Moderate resistance, standing.
1 minute		Moderate resistance, sitting.
30 seconds		Moderate resistance, standing.
2 minutes		Add more resistance, sitting.
3 minutes	1 song	Light resistance with a spin of the legs.
3 minutes	2 songs	Moderate resistance, sitting.
1 minute		Add a bit more resistance, sitting.
1 minute		Add a bit more resistance, sitting.
1 minute		Add a bit more resistance, sitting.
1 minute	1 song	Heavy resistance, standing.

1 minute	1 song	Add resistance, sitting.
1 minute		Add resistance, standing to the top of the hill.
20 seconds	1 song	Decrease resistance, sprint.
20 seconds		Active rest, easy spin.
30 seconds		Sprint.
30 seconds		Active rest, easy spin.
45 seconds		Sprint.
4 minutes	1 song	Recover and cool down, stretch.

Glossary

Cadence – Revolutions per minute of pedal stroke.

Jump/lift up and down – A short, quick burst of speed.

Leg speed – How fast one can turn the cranks; measured in revolutions per minute (rpms).

Paceline – Group of riders in a line, alternating turns pulling to the front and sitting in.

Rollers – Stationary training device composed of three cylindrical tubes (rollers) on which a bicycle sits.

Spin – Often used to mean high cadence; more accurately refers to the fluidity or suppleness of the pedal stroke.

Sprint – Acceleration to a high speed.

Trainer – A stationary training device. Rollers, Lifecycles, and Turbo Trainers are all varieties of stationary trainers.

Tempo – Pace; normally implies hard, steady riding.

Index

A

American College of
    Obstetricians and
    Gynecologists (ACOG), 38
ankling pattern, 6, 7
antihypertensive agents, 37
arched back, 19
arm extension, 14
arthritis, 40-41

B

back, 19, 36
back stretch, 45
beta blockers, 37
biceps femoris, 4
bike, set-up, 12-14
blood glucose testing, 39
blood, peripheral pooling, 37
body alignment cues, 32, 42
body positioning, 16-18
bottom dead center, 4
bottoming out, 39
brake pad, 13
breaks, postural, 34, 36, 39, 41
breathing, 33
Burke, E., 6, 14
buttocks, sore, 36

C

cadence, 1, 34, 41
calcium channel blockers, 37
calf stretch, 44
carbohydrates, 40

chest stretch, 46
class components/formats, 42-51
cleansing breath, 49
cleats, 6, 9, 10, 11, 38
climbing, 20-21
clipless pedals, 6, 10
closed and center hand position,
    16, 19
clothing, 9, 10, 30, 35
cool-down, 33, 37, 40, 42, 43, 49,
    50, 51
cross training, 30
cueing, 32-33
Cycle Reebok™, 2

D

dehydration, 37
diabetes, 39-40
diuretics, 37
dorsiflexion, 6

E

electromyography (EMG), 4
emergency brake, 40
endurance workout, 48-49
equipment, 9-14
ergometers, 1

F

feet, sore, 36
fixed-pedal systems, 6

flats, 18-20
floating-pedal systems, 6
flywheel resistance dial, 35
footwear, 9-10, 35
form. *see* position; spinal
  alignment

G

gastrocnemius, 5, 6
gloves, 10
gluteus maximus, 4, 5
Goldberg, Johnny, 1-2
graded exercise test, 37
Gregor, Robert, 4, 6
grip, 18, 20, 35

H

hamstring stretch, 43
hamstrings, 4, 5
hand positions, 16-18, 19, 41, 42
handlebars, 13, 14, 35
hands, numb, 35-36
heart rate, 36, 37
heart rate monitors, 33-34
hill work. *see* climbing
hip extension, 4, 5
hip flexion, 5
hydration, 34, 37, 38
hyperglycemia, 40
hypertension, 37-38
hypoglycemia, 38
hypotension, 37

I

iliacus, 5
indoor cycling, growth and
  benefits of, 2-3

injury prevention, 34-36
intensity
  and participants with medical
    conditions, 36, 37
  monitoring, 33-34
intervals, 50

J

Johnny G. *see* Goldberg, Johnny
joint function, 41
jump/lift up and down, 30-32,
  48, 49, 52

K

Keiser, 2
kinesiology, 4-8
knee extension, 4, 5, 6
knee flexion, 4, 5, 6
knee hyperextension, 39

L

lactic acid, 3
lateral hip stretch, 47
leg speed, 26, 52
lifts, 30-32, 48, 49, 52
LOOK cleats, 9, 11
lumbar lordosis, 39

M

Mad Dogg Athletics. *see*
  Spinning®
maximum heart rate, 37
medical conditions, 36-41
mixed terrain workout, 50-51
modifications, 36, 37

monitoring, intensity, 33-34
mountain biking, 2
muscle focus, 32-33
music, 30, 42, 49

N

Nichols, Jeanne, 41
numb hands, 35-36

O

off-road cycling, 8
one-legged drills, 24
osteoarthritis, 40
outdoor cycling, 2, 30

P

paceline, 50, 52
padded cycling shorts, 9, 35
pedal crank speed, 40
pedal position, 4, 6
pedal stroke, 1, 3, 6, 8
  climbing, 20
  sprints, 22
pedaling technique, 14-15
pedals, 13
personal limitations, 36-41
plantar flexion, 6, 8
pop pins, 12
position
  for sprints, 23
  for standing climb, 29
  for standing jog, 27
  for standing on a flat, 25
  improper, 26, 28, 29, 32
  to stand and sit, lift, or
    jump, 31
  see also spinal alignment

postural alignment cues, 32, 42
postural breaks, 34, 36, 39, 41
Power Pacing™, 2
power phase. see propulsion
  phase
preferred cadence, 41
pregnancy, 38-39
profile, 42, 43
programming, 42-51
propulsion phase, 4, 6, 8
psoas major, 5
psoas minor, 5
pulling back, 15

Q

quadriceps stretch, 45

R

range-of-motion exercises, 41
rating of perceived exertion
  (RPE), 33, 37, 38
recovery phase, 4, 8
rectus femoris, 4, 5
Reebok™, 2
relaxation techniques, 20
resistance control knob, 13, 35
rheumatoid arthritis, 40, 41
rollers, 1, 52
rounded back, 19

S

saddle, 13
safety, 3, 34-36, 40, 42
Schwinn®, 2
seat positioning, 14
seated positions
  climbing, 20-21

flats, 18-20
one-legged drills, 24
sprints, 22-24
semimembranosus, 4, 5
shoe strap, 14
shoelaces, 9-10, 40
shoes, 9-10, 35
SPD cleats, 9, 11
spin, 49, 50, 51, 52
spinal alignment
    climbing, 21
    improper, 19, 22, 24, 29
sprinting, 23
Spinning®, 2
Sporting Goods Manufacturing
    Association, 2
sprint, 1, 22-24, 48, 50, 51, 52
standing positions
    stand and sit, lift, or jump,
        30-32, 48, 49, 52
    standing climb, 28-29
    standing jog/run/sprint, 26-27
    standing on a flat, 25, 48
stationary bikes, 1
stopping, 35
strength training, 6
strength workout, 49-50
stress injuries, 12
stretching, 34, 41, 43-47,
    49, 50, 51
Studio Cycling. see Cycle Reebok
swaying, 2

T

teaching techniques, 30, 40
technique, cycling
body positioning, 16-18
pedaling, 14-15
seated positions, 18-24
standing positions, 25-32
tempo, 42, 52

tension dial, 13, 35
toe clips, 4
top dead center, 4, 6
towels, 35
trainers, 1, 52
triceps stretch, 47
troubleshooting, 35-36
type 1 diabetes, 39-40
type 2 diabetes, 39

U

upstroke. see recovery phase

V

vasodilators, 37
vastus lateralis, 4, 5
vastus medialis, 4, 5
venous return, 3
ventilation, 12, 34, 40
verbal cues, 32
visualization, 33
$\dot{V}O_2$ max, 1, 36
Voight, Karen, 2

W

warm-up, 40, 42, 48, 49, 50
water, 34, 37
water bottle, 10
water bottle cage, 13
workload, 1
    for participants with
        arthritis, 41
    for pregnant participants, 38

References and Suggested Reading

American Council on Exercise. (1997). *Personal Trainer Manual.* San Diego, CA.

American College of Obstetricians and Gynecologists (ACOG). (1994). *ACOG Technical Bulletin,* 189.

American College of Sports Medicine (ASCM). (1995). *ACSM's Guidelines for Exercise Testing and Prescription,* 5th edition. Baltimore: Williams and Wilkins.

Burke, E. (1986). *Science of Cycling.* Champaign, Ill.: Human Kinetics.

Burke, E. (1995). *Serious Cycling.* Champaign, Ill.: Human Kinetics.

Burke, E. (1996). *High-Tech Cycling.* Champaign, Ill.: Human Kinetics.

Burke, E. (1998). *Cycling Health and Physiology.* College Park, Md.: Vitesse Press.

Durstine, L. & Pate, R. (1993). Cardiorespiratory responses to acute exercise. In *ACSM's Resource Manual for Guidelines for Exercise Testing and Prescription,* 2nd ed. Philadelphia: Lea & Febiger.

Howley, E. & Franks, B. (1992). *Health Fitness Instructor's Handbook.* Champaign, Ill.: Human Kinetics.

McArdle, W., Katch, F., & Katch, V. (1986). *Exercise Physiology: Energy, Nutrition and Human Performance,* 2nd ed. Philadelphia, Penn.: Lea and Febiger.

Phinney, D. & Carpenter, C. (1992). *Training for Cycling.* New York City: Berkeley Publishing Group.

Ruderman, N. & Devlin, J. (1997). *Health Professional's Guide to Diabetes and Exercise.* American Diabetes Association.

Shechtman, N. & Perdew, L. (1998). *Indoor Cycling Basics Home Study Course.* Irvine, Cal.: NRS Consulting.

Stavig, A., Francis, P., & Buono, M. (1998). Physiologic response to a typical studio cycling session. *ACSM's Health and Fitness Journal.*

Whaley, M., Kaminsky, L., Dwyer, G., Getchell, L., & Norton, J. (1992). Questioning the routine use of 220–AGE heart rate formula. *Medicine & Science in Sports & Exercise,* 24, 1173.

NOTES

NOTES

NOTES

NOTES

NOTES

NOTES

ABOUT THE AUTHOR

Norma Shechtman has been involved in the fitness industry for more than 20 years. She holds master's degrees in education and kinesiology. She is an ACE-certified Personal Trainer and Group Fitness Instructor, as well as NASM, AFAA, and USWFA certified. Shechtman has authored books, video and audio tapes, and magazine and newspaper articles. She has been featured on ESPN, cable television, infomercials, and numerous videos, and also wrote the *ACE Personal Trainer Home Study Program*. In 1999, Shechtman won an award of distinction from *The Communication Awards* for her "Cycling Basics" video.

SPONSOR

going the extra mile.

Best known for the #1 selling commercial treadmill in the world, Star Trac offers a complete line of high quality, cardiovascular fitness equipment including elliptical trainers, stationary bikes, and stair climbers. The company also offers Trekking™ and Precision Cycling™, two of the hottest group exercise programs on the market today. Every day, more than 2 million people in over 65 countries use Star Trac cardiovascular exercise equipment in fitness facilities and at home. Call 1-800-228-6635 or visit the company's web site at www.startrac.com

To locate this or any other ACE-approved continuing education provider in your area, call ACE at (800) 825-3636 and ask for Professional Services, or visit our course locator at www.acefitness.org under "I'm Certified."

SPONSOR

KEISER®

Keiser is a continuing education provider for the American Council on Exercise. Its ACE-approved workshops, including the six-hour Power Pacer/Freewheeling Instructor Certification Workshop, will give you the skills you need to teach safe and effective group indoor cycling classes and provide ACE continuing education credits toward your certification renewal. Keiser is constantly developing new education options to help you maintain up-to-date knowledge and become a better instructor.

Keiser Corporation
2470 S. Cherry Avenue
Fresno, CA   93706

Toll-free: (800) 888-7009
Telephone: (559) 256-8000
Fax: (559) 256-8100

Web site: www.keiser.com

E-mail: info@keiser.com

To locate this or any other ACE-approved continuing education provider in your area, call ACE at (800) 825-3636 and ask for Professional Services, or visit our course locator at www.acefitness.org under "I'm Certified."